Afloat, Atop a Marbled Sea

ISBN: 978-0-9785353-4-6

This book is dedicated to my family:

Immediate:

Jerry

Greta

Kareem

Kadiya

Kristen

Kiba

Extended:

Through blood

Through friendship

Through geography

Through readership

-Kenyada Meadows

Contents

Foreword
by Linda LeBlanc

Kahlil Gibran wrote, "Poetry is a deal of joy and pain and wonder, with a dash of the dictionary."

Kenyada Meadows is a poet in the truest sense of the word. His work embodies all of those emotions. They radiate from the page with extraordinary imagery and rhythm. In Letter in a Bottle, one feels the quiet, the floating. "Afloat, atop smooth orange seas and glistening in the setting sun. No clouds. No waves. No boats. No breeze. No warmth. No sounds. No birds. No one." When we arrived at, No one, we experience the total silence and solitude. A subtle rhythm has led us there.

Kenyada writes not only of the joy of love, but also the pain and fear. In doing so, he is a master of the metaphor. In Stay, a heart "broke free of its leash and made a dash for the busy streets...a giddy heart off its leash." What a delightful image. The heart's owner then orders it to Heel and Stay but feels "helpless, an observer who's run out of commands." In Hummingbirds, "Hearts just want to be hummingbirds, zipping, flitting around and about. Unbridled." Yet Kenyada asks if the wings of the heart should be clipped or should it fly around from chest to chest, "even at the risk of broken wings?" In another poem, love is a stallion, silent and strong. "And you do gallop and you do prance about, and there is joy. What a ride." But at the same time, "You do buck, and you do kick. And there is fear." In Fun and Games, "Hearts bounce around on trampolines...until something gives. Breaks. Tears."

This sense of loss weaves through many of the poems. Columbus-Take Two. "They keep sellin' off the islands, all the land...Their paradise, not yours...Where you used to swim and play. Where you used to know. Now you only go." In History Rewritten, Repeated, Kenyada uses a pencil to make his point. "Still sharp, but the eraser done down to the quick. Island chain smudged together. Shorelines eroded erased... Rubbing the country out, till there is a hole in it." A great image appears in the poem Machete when he refers to it as the "Haitian Excalibur... Gone from cutting weed and chappin' bush limb by limb, to chappin' enemy and friend...Costin' this country an arm and a leg."

Afloat, Atop a Marbled Sea

Poetry is like magic in that what you see is not always as it seems. We all interpret based on what we've experienced and how we feel. It Used To Be Fridays talks of getting a toy on Fridays. "I would be infatuated with its novelty but not in love. Rarely in long lasting love. Because every week had a Friday. Merely a crush until the next toy came my way." But then Kenyada asks, "Suppose there were no more? No more toys... And no more chances. And no more love?" Is he truly speaking of toys or perhaps relationships? In Torn, is he writing about a piece of paper or humanity? "A piece of paper, blank, and new, now tattered up and tattooed too. A tortured soul, once smooth when born, now dusty, dirty, ragged, torn."

Gibran said "with a dash of the dictionary." Kenyada's poems resonate with powerful verbs such as those in the poem Mona Lisa where he describes crowds who've come to view the worn out old lady. "Voyeurs glare, snapping away, rape her with their eyes. They salivate and digest her, white teeth snapping and flashing, tearing and burning through her, frothing and licking, ruining, ravaging her, savaging her." Writing doesn't get any stronger than that.

In Steel Drums, one can almost feel them vibrating. "Flung as widely as the maestro's arms can swing...Four-legged percussionists liberating drums, beating everything out. Wild and rabid composers."

There are short fun impressions in Getting Antsy, Rummy Mummy, Rotisserie Chicken, Too Sweet Tea and The Neighbor's Boy. But in Glass Vault, Kenyada writes of what most of us probably experience at some time. "Through walls of glass I see inside, what otherwise I'd wish to hide. Good things not done, bad things I said... I'm clearly trapped by my regret." Then he's set free in Uprooted. "I am pulling up, stretching out... No longer waist deep. Limber and free. Advancing now, gliding along the surface, Refreshed. Breathing deeply. Walking on water." The alliteration in Walking on water conveys an airy feeling that lifts us and we no longer feel earthbound.

Thus with his rare insight into the world and the human psyche, Kenyada transcends us to another place and inspires us to look inside ourselves to discover our own joy and pain.

Foreword

by Obediah Michael Smith

Kenyada certainly does make visual art with his words. This is
evident in the first line of the first poem in this collection:

"Afloat, atop smooth orange seas and glistening in the setting sun."

In the line that follows, that completes his first two-line stanza,
how delicious is his syntax and how lovely and original is his rhythm:

"No clouds. No waves. No boats. No breeze. No warmth. No sounds.
No birds. No one."

That you are in for a cinematographic treat from the outset is obvious.
The challenge Kenyada takes on is certainly what art is about-to
elevate to the level of symbol what is ordinary or what are
everyday things and everyday happenings. A treat certainly, when
it succeeds. You sigh, rewarded. To read each poem is to watch
what he picks up or picks on to translate into art object-what he
chooses to make the subject of his art. Will it translate you ask and
when it does, what deep satisfaction.

Those that provide the deepest satisfaction-those that I love |3
best are those without verbiage as was Van Gogh's aim at a high
point of his painting in the South of France-as he explained to his
brother Theo in a letter-to avoid giving any space at all to what was
superfluous. It is this paradox you see: words being your medium
and desiring to use words in a way that the words put down-the
words comprising the poem-are not thought of when read. Just as
standing at a window to look out and the scene beyond is the focus
not the glass. The very same being true of glasses we wear. The idea
is that they would make our vision clear. We do not wear glasses to
focus upon the lenses. When we do, our prescription is wrong or our
glasses are smudged and require cleaning.

In which poems in this collection is Kenyada's vision clearest?
In which poems is there not a single word that gets in the way?
Here is my list: "A Beautiful Heart," "Uprooted," "Torn," "The
Neighbour's Boy," "Machete," "Fun and Games," "Stay!" "Never
Leaned to Land," "Rainmaker," "Glass Vault" and there are others
as well but these are the ones I favor most.

Kenyada is well aware of the need to keep the lines fresh–to keep the words flowing fresh and his well crafted lines most often do succeed. His vocabulary and his knowledge of grammar guarantee the avoidance of overused words and phrases.

His is a house certainly in which I'd request a glass of water and drink it entirely comfortably and empty the glass. There are those houses we visit and even if offered water we decline. Not trusting, we find some excuse to refuse even water if offered.

These poems of Kenyada's, in this collection, are mostly fresh–are mostly refreshing. What he brings into art–into poetry–what he selects is mostly so very original: his angles of observation–his slant or take on things–his snapshots of life.

Art is aimed at with every image and in every line and is far more often than not, attained. As in "Zen in the Art of Archery," it is entirely all right to miss. What is important with each line is to stretch the bow as it were until it is as taut as you'd stretch it. You then release it, letting IT shoot, as Zen master, Awa Kenzô insisted, in explaining the process to Eugen Herrigel, his archery student, the German philosophy professor and author.

Kenyada knows a lot about making art or about allowing himself to be made by art which are two ends of the same dynamic. I like when he hits his target therefore as well as when he misses. He hits it often enough certainly for my money and for my taste. He hits it often enough to challenge and to inspire my own art making effort and my engagement in artistic life.

The standard he sets with what he accomplishes in these poems in this collection, far more often than not, tells me–tells any serious poet that to compete you will have to keep your pencils sharp as well as your game as well your art. This certainly is the dynamic necessary to keep the literary arts–nationally and regionally and in the world, alive and advancing.

Letter in a Bottle:

Afloat, atop smooth orange seas and glistening in the setting sun.
No clouds. No waves. No boats. No breeze. No warmth. No sounds.
No birds. No one.

A bottle, fragile as a shell; a note inside more fragile yet.
Safeguarded in the bottle well, and from the ocean's teardrops wet.

Though sweat and blood and tears and such, mix with the ink
to form these lines.
Now rising from the ocean's clutch to breathe fresh air, to speak
their minds.

About my love, about my heart and other things I put at stake.
Why did I say "Let's be apart," "I need some space." "Let's take a break.?"

Like grains of sand in currents deep, just through and just beyond
my grip.
You've turned away. I was asleep. I woke too late. The grains have
slipped.

You are the sun and spring time's flair and golden leaves,

White mountain caps.
I love your skin, I love your hair; your stubbornness one day, perhaps.

Or let it sink and let it go, and let us put this in the past.
And start anew; let patience flow through hearts so big, so full, so vast.

Uncork the bottle. Break its spell. Let feelings out. Let sadness flee.
Let's break this hold, start living well. So set our minds and set
them free.

But...

If you hate these words, if they say nil or leave you bare and
don't sound right.
Do as you would and as you will, and throw them back into the
night...

Queen's Gambit:

Buzzing restaurant tables, dimly lit
Dark squares on a chess board.
A quiet game is about to begin,
Has already begun perhaps, with a preemptive strike.
A bold opening, to send out the queen.
A queen who perhaps sent out herself,
As a queen might.

As a queen would,
Tall, stately, elegant, intoxicatingly regal.
Perhaps icy.
An unknown, potentially dangerous queen,
Having slaughtered perhaps many, perhaps few.
Floating, breezing across the middle of the board.
Not looking, having already seen.

A wasted move?
Or part of a bigger plan, perhaps.
6| Perhaps a plot, even.

Almost disappearing toward the edge of the board now,
To observe the action,
Or even to console the careless and captured pieces no longer in play,
Huddled together along the fringes.
Pieces of the past to be left behind.
But not forgotten.
We respect the past, but can not live vigilantly in it.

Check.

She seems to move with concern, though; even for the pawn.
Working with her pieces.
Her brethren who perish, even figuratively.

An unknown queen, yes.
But perhaps a king and queen could take a chance
And meet in the middle.
Of any board. Of every board.
Perhaps she is not the enemy, after all.

Love, You Are a Stallion:

Love, you are a stallion,
Silent and strong.
Smooth black coat glistening in the enduring sunlight,
Absorbing warmth for those who choose to sit on your full back.
Broad shoulders, thick neck ready for the weight,
To bear my burdens with me and for me.
And you do gallop and you do prance about,
And there is joy.
What a ride.

Chiseled jaw, noble face, well-built and still.
Your breath is even, velvet and fit.
An inviting smile,
Tender it would seem...
From the outside looking in...

Love, you are a stallion,
Bitter and strong.
Smooth black coat fighting the torturous sun.
Equally hot and burning for those strapped to your full back.
The cogs of your shoulders grind against your granite neck,
And you do buck, and you do kick,
And there is fear.
And your muscles flex until your coat becomes oily and slick.
Hard to stay put, the options are few.
What a ride.

Clenched jaw, angry face, built for the fight,
And fighting still.
Your breath is jagged and foul,
You salivate from the exertion and the thought of pain
A smirk between heaves,
Or so it would seem...
From the ground, looking up from one's broken back.

A Beating Heart:

A big heart that beats,
And beats,
And beats in me,
And on me,
And on my sleeve.
And beats me down,
And up.

A big heart that beats,
And beats,
And beats in me,
And sucks me in,
And swallows me up,
And whole.

And beats.
And beats.

8|

It Used to Be Fridays:

I used to get toys on Fridays.
Most Fridays.
Sometimes it would be Saturday.

I would love it for a while.
Mostly on the shelf.
I would love it on the shelf in the store,
Because it wasn't mine.

But then it would be.
And then I would be infatuated with its novelty
But not in love.
Rarely in long-lasting love.
Because every week had a Friday.
Or Saturday.

Merely a crush.
Until the next toy came my way.
Then it would be crushed under the weight of broken and forgotten toys
And broken hearts of toys that came my way. |9

But others would love my toys
Mostly on my shelf
And they would love it on my shelf in my room
In my toy box.
In my room.

I liked my toys. Never loved my toys
Because there would always be more Fridays,
And if not, Saturdays.
I never thought, "What if there were no more half-days in primary
school on Friday?"

And no more trips to the store?
But only playing with toys littering my room and strewn on my floor?
Even the broken ones...
Suppose... there were no more?"

No more toys....
And no more half days...
And no more chances...
And no more love...

Afloat, Atop a Marbled Sea

Mango Skin:

So much to lose,
Sealed tight within.
Won't let it bruise,
That mango skin.
So juicy,
Firm;
So round and fun.
Sweet paradise,
In every one.

Uprooted:

I am pulling up, stretching out.
Uprooting;
Like a barefooted ballerina,
Advancing on pale, slender toes.
Skirt hoisted, tiptoeing out of the muck;
No longer waist deep.
Limber and free.
Advancing now, gliding along the surface,
Refreshed.
Breathing deeply.
Walking on water.

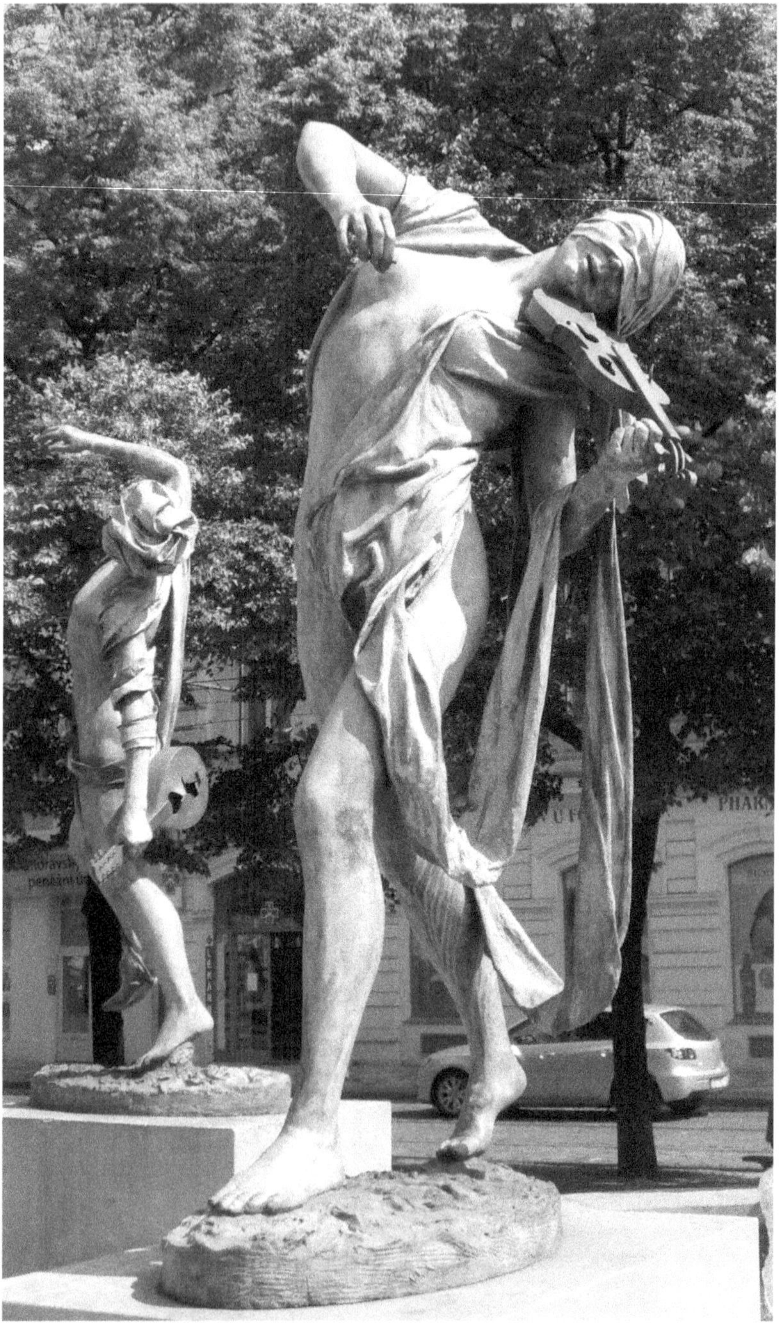

Afloat, Atop a Marbled Sea

Torn:

In a lonely courtyard, blown around
Swept up, up high, dashed to the ground.
A tortured soul, once smooth when born,
Now dusty, dirty, ragged, torn.

A piece of paper, blank and new,
Now tattered up and tattooed too.
Flash-dancing to the windy whims
Of fragile, wobbly, battered limbs.

To keep up such a frantic pace,
Would be unstable and unsafe.
It's paper thin, its ashen hue,
Like veins exposed, so old and blue.

With fading words since each line bleeds,
It does not make sense how it reads.
It's lost its voice, it cannot speak.
It's limp and feeble, old and weak.

| 13

Gets blown around against the wind,
Against its wishes, walled and pinned.
It seems that it just can't go on...
Then just like that, it's up and gone...

Rummy Mummy:

She said your father used to drink,
Now she wants you to stop it.
She thinks it runs in your genes,
And rum's in your jeans pocket.

14|

Getting Antsy:

If ants were people
They would be at the airport
In long lines.
They race here in long lines
To crawl there in long lines
Stopping and going
To-ing and fro-ing
But all in a line.
Racing, marching, rolling
In a rush
Onto what they heard was sweet on the other side.

|15

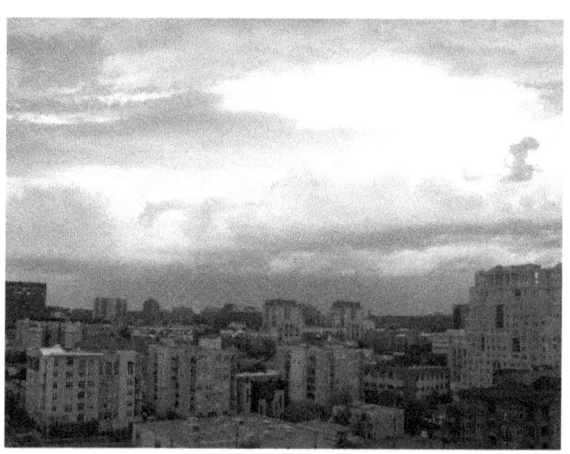

Afloat, Atop a Marbled Sea

Supernova:

The morning creeps up on me,
Upon me;
Like a thief in the night bent on molestation.
Always with tiptoeing care and quiet.
So slowly at first that it seems to stand still.
But by the time that its light is too bright to veil any longer under
its star studded cloak of darkness;
After having strangled a much smaller, weaker moon;
It springs!
It just springs it on me blindingly,
With blaring alarm...

The Tears of Whales:

After each meal,
He burps his complaint.
He can't eat anymore,
And not for a lack of trying.
His stomach hurts.
And it was good.
And in not too long it will be bad.

Eager tears deprived of a full journey.
His tightly cloaked gut shading the floor,
Greedily soaks them up.
Keeping it dry.

His tears come.
Quietly at first.
Then the slobbering,
And my disdain.

We both subtly, slowly shake our heads.
Look out the window
In search of distance.
Not finding it is just as well.
The sea is made of tears of whales.

The Rumble in Row 22:

I nod my head. I cross my feet.
Though wide awake, I am discreet.

I have my left. You have your right,
Though in between–we meet, we fight.

We fight through quiet skies of blue.
Red corner–me, Blue corner–you.

Though eyes are closed,
Our minds' eyes meet.
You're in my space; your hands, your feet.

You think you'll win.
I disagree. Fight to the death.
I'll win–you'll see.

Planes' engines rumble.
Oh yes they do;
But not like us in 22...

|19

The Neighbor's Boy:

Poor little boy you are the worst enemy to yourself.
Stop thrown' things, stop breakin' things, stop climbin' on the shelf,
Stop screamin' and stop scribblin', stop swingin' on the door,
And you better soon stop cryin', fore they give you somethin' to cry for.

Rotisserie Chicken:

What was once
Peacocking,
Prancing,
Crowing,
Waxed,
Glistening,
Glowing.
Now plucked,
Defeathered,
Exposed to the weather.
Baked.
Stripped.
The whirring sounds of the pit crew.
Pitchforks,
Picking.
Chomping.
Doors pried off,
Stripped down to the bone,
Gutted.
Bare frame,
Down to the plates.
Just Greasy,
Oil stains.

Kamikaze Angels:

Every millimeter of its journey from the heavens,
A new wish.
Perhaps they will dance and splash about,
Like fallen angels to soften our hard earth.
A lifetime.
Kamikaze.
Selfless, hopeless, one by one;
Hopeful that the snowflake causes the avalanche.
Every body-length of each drop of rain,
Writhing,
Screaming on its way down.
A battle cry,
Or proof of fear.
Sweating.
Wetting itself.
Crying for the end to come,
For the end is near.
For centuries,
Each drop tries to fertilize this third egg from the sun.
Fossilized.
Hardened shell.
Yielding perhaps just a little moss.

Mona Lisa:

The dignity of the lady is not well preserved.
Voyeurs glare through,
Congregate around her open window.
Snapping away, just short of snapping her up.
If only they could.
Their hands are too short.
So they rape her with their eyes,
In their hearts,
In the tight, inescapable quarters of their dark, stench-ridden minds,
No one seems to mind,
Not even her.
Not so much.

Like a prostitute, so used to being ogled, consumed
By savages
Who claim to respect, to revere her
They salivate and digest her
Holding up their tools of consumption
White teeth snapping and flashing
Tearing and burning through her
Merely seconds in between
The sounds of snapping and clicking, frothing, licking
Ruining, ravaging her
Savaging her,
The conquest of it,
Then bragging about the art of it
Bragging about it to their friends
The irony captured for eternity in paint and film.
Memories and words.

Security stands by merely watching the illicit
Complicit.
Decriminalized brutality against this worn out, old woman.

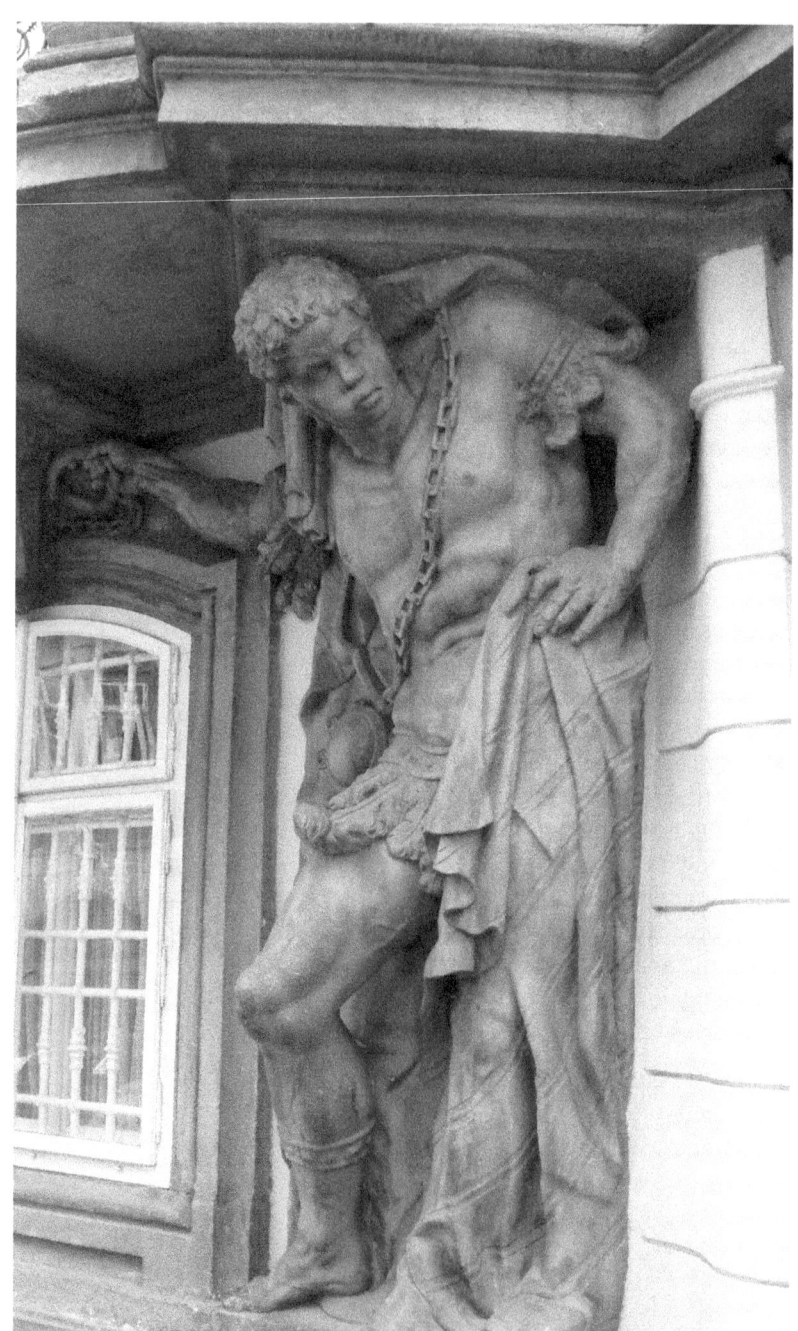

24|

Afloat, Atop a Marbled Sea

Fields of Iniquity:

The sound of drum beats in the air
Beat in my eardrums
Thick, sombre branches of trees
Fertile soils irrigated with sweat
Steamy, tropical branches
From which children who wanted to play all day
could swing
From which adults who were reluctant to give way
could swing

Dark knights with clenched, uplifted fists
Pale days hooded with blindly white rays
Fair shot versus all shot
Supreme, absolute equality
No shot
Presupposition of equality

Self-imposed caste systems on like groups abound
Race...
To religious differences as a means to dictate
Run...
To socio-economics as a way to further discriminate

Still fight for gray, neither black nor white
Never give in
Equality.
Never give inequality fertile soil.

Play and swing all day on branches
Uproot and cut away such branches
Callous, indifferent branches.

26|

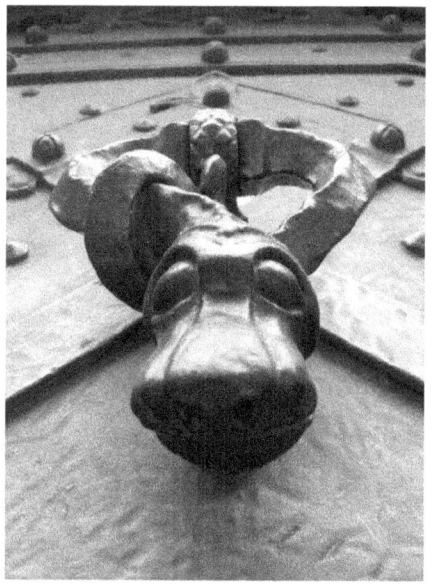

Afloat, Atop a Marbled Sea

The Big House:

Can't wait to go work in the big house.
In a league, on an island of its own.
Get out this sun.
It beats working in the sun, chappin' bush.

Shiny and nice.
Could never live there, stay there.
But we could clean there,
Do our dealings there,
Work there.

It is work, and that's good.
But what if the big house went away
And the masters stopped flying in
Swooping down,
Then what?

What of the hands, and crops, and bartering, and trades?
No trading, few known trades.
Just work in the big house.
Big work.
Step out from behind the asses and ploughs.
Explore, plough your own path.

|27

See the big house for what it is.
Better than nothing.
But not a privilege,
But for the few.
Its time for us to knock off.
Get off and out.

Sweatshop:

No more straw to chew on
'Cause in the market its gone
Bahamian crafts in the past
Now its made in taiwan

No shame in the game they play
No more slavin' they say
Make more money each day
'Straw market'? 'Straw Man'–either way

Feel free not to weave
But feel free to believe
Weave ourselves in a knot
The sweatshop just gettin' hot.

Columbus–Take Two:

They keep sellin' off the islands,
All the land, even the islands and cays..
Like ships selling off their anchors
So that they can drift off,
Nod off.
Gatta be asleep at the wheel.
Runnin' aground
On these other people land.

Their paradise, not yours, but you could go work there.
Where you used to swim and play.
Where you used to know.
Now you only go.
For now.
Definitely not your paradise.
Not any more than a slave centuries ago basked in the Bahamian sun,
Layin' around
In paradise.

|29

All that beautiful sand in your hair,
In your eyes,
In your face.
Soon need to throw tokens to walk in your own lil piece a yard.
If it's even your yard.
If you even have a place,
Somewhere to call home.

History Rewritten, Repeated:

Brand new pencil long as a nail
But the eraser done down to the quick.
Each letter, islands smudged together
Shorelines eroded.
No margin.

Every new government
Overwriting the other
Overriding the other
Robbing the country
Rubbing the country out
Til there's a hole in it.

Clear Blue Freedom and a Purple Wake:

They have baited the line.
No longer tied around our necks,
Cutting into our breath and our backs,
Binding our wrists.
The lines are thinner now,
Much harder to see.
Especially in the dark,
In the perpetual night.

They have let us run even farther; however,
Than the razor sharp point at which we were baited and hooked,
At which we sank our teeth ambitiously in.

Free, we climb.
We swim through the clear blue freedom,
Until the line jerks down against our weight,
Until it reminds us of tethers and limits,
And the taste of our own bloody mouths.

Abruptly we are reeled backwards,
If not all the way in,
If not all the way dead.
Blue, not all the way clear,
Leaving behind a purple wake.

|31

No longer required to bow down,
Step down,
And step aside,
We thought.

They have ground on which to stand.
We without forty acres or even one,
Just a narrow path,
Treacherous, but ours.
A path generally to a familiar lot and station.

But we also have ground to stand, though treacherous should we
stand it.
On which to walk,

Stand,
And stand our ground.
In theory.

A ground on which we often lay dead.
Sometimes at our own hands,
But too often by those on neighborhood safari,
And those without sympathy for the truly endangered.
Those who would out-arm nature,
Then complain of the sharp teeth and tusks they themselves eagerly,
And illegally pursued.

They are those who would shoot
And quiet screams.
They are those who would defend.
They are those who would free and walk free.
Bloodshed and blood guilt the only proof that they were ever here.

Besides of course, the bodies left lying in their wake,
In sticky blood,
And sweets going sticky in the wet,
In the dark, perpetual night.

Tension on the Line:

Pulled too tight.
Ideas below the surface
Moving 'round
Different sizes and depths
Not learned in a school.

Easy to see though
Just deeper than we often like to go.
Easier than fish in a barrel
Swimming 'round
Getting fat
Delicious to hook into.
Careful bringing them to the surface
To the tip of my tongue.

|33

Steel Drums:

Melodies of trash strewn across the street
Notes of decay strum themselves into the air
Flung as widely as the maestro's arms can swing
As far as sound will blow them.
Four-legged percussionists liberating drums
Beating everything out.
Wild and rabid composers,
Dragging out every note.

Too Sweet Tea:

Grains of sugar at the bottom of a too sweet tea.
Stray dogs swirl about,
Twirl about.
Chasing their tails
Round and round.

Eventually slowing, settling down.
Lying around
And about.
Collapsing in a saturated heap.

Afloat, Atop a Marbled Sea

Fun and Games:

Hearts bounce around on trampolines.
Backflips and twists and sommersaults.
Young. Invincible. Reckless. Laughing.
It's all fun and games,
Until something gives,
Breaks.
Tears.

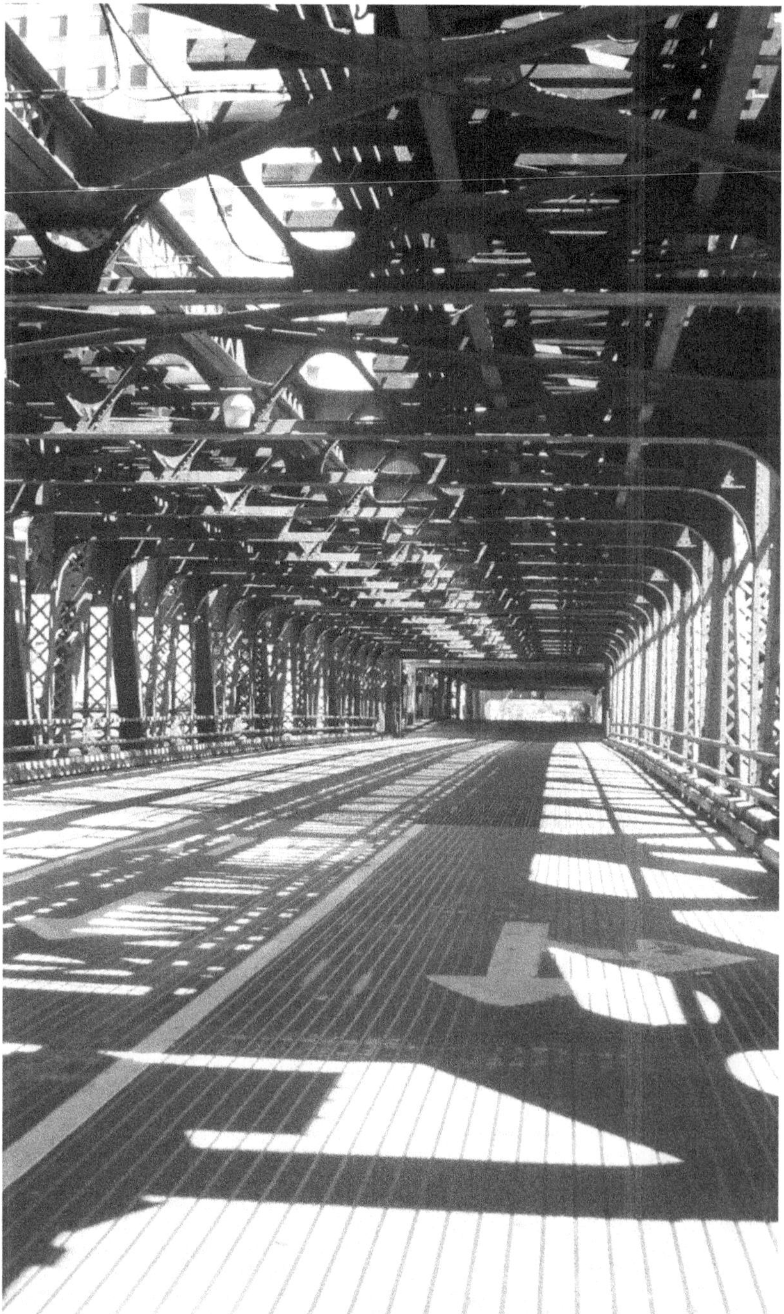

38|

Afloat, Atop a Marbled Sea

Stay!!:

I thought my heart was happy.
Until it broke free of its leash and made a dash for the busy streets,
Full of drunken bicycles, vendors, people bumping into each other;
And lunatic drivers who seldom brake,
Who would never notice a giddy heart off its leash.

A heart that typically responds to even a whisper,
To sit or play dead.
I told it to heel.
I told it to "STAY!"

But I think,
I feel,
I am a helpless owner.
An observer,
Who's run out of commands...

|39

Hummingbirds:

They don't properly know how to be free.
Hearts just want to be hummingbirds,
Zipping, flitting around and about.
Unbridled, unruly, left to their own devices,
If they'd give it even that much thought.

But they need cages.
To be ribbed.
Girdled.

They need muzzles to stop their chirping,
Shackles to stop their pollenating as they wish,
To weigh them down.
They need straightjackets to stop them from thrashing,
Tethers to stop them from smashing,
To stop them from crashing, burning,
Breaking.

40|

Never Learned to Land:

But should the wings of the heart be clipped at all?
Even its feathers ruffled,
Its song muffled?
Is it humane to cage this bird?
Sensible?
Possible?

Should it fly around from chest to chest,
From nest to nest?
On wind to wind,
And crazily and blindly?
Wildly clawing at things?
Grasping at straws?

Even at the risk of broken wings?
Broken hearts?
To find its flock, birds of a feather,
To find its mate?

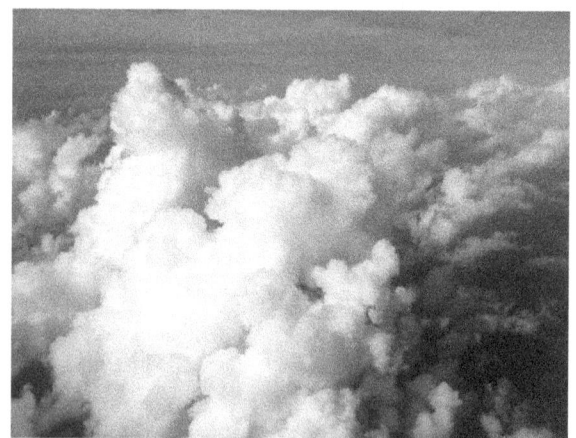

Afloat, Atop a Marbled Sea

Rainmaker:

You have seeded the clouds in me.
You have inspired in me a rainstorm,
A rushing flow,
A waterfall,
A deluge of poetry;
To wash myself clean and free with,
To wash myself away with.

Time Burning Away:

Every second a spark
Growing into a minute flame
Small enough, easy to snuff
Immaterial little flame
Blazing weekly, never weakly

But heat will remain
Sparks rekindle that flame
Laying waste to soot covered hourglasses
Veils of smoke conceal the little time left

Time burns away dryly,
Blazing now
An unstoppable conflagration,
Raging now
Never weakly,
Insatiable as hell
The inextinguishable wick,
Tick, tick, ticking us off
Burning as steady as clockwork...

Glass Vault:

Through vaulted glass I see inside
What otherwise, I'd wish to hide
Good things not done, bad things I've said,
Bad things I've done stay in my head.
Stay on my mind–it is my fault,
Stay on a shelf, inside the vault.

Walls of glass get thick with time,
Yet free of dust, and free of grime
Each fossilized disparity,
Roped-off; showcased with clarity.
I turn around to freedom, yet;
I'm clearly trapped by my regret...

Though other things I may forget;
In clear contrast to my regret...

Versus Verses:

The world is not a poem
Comprised of well-manicured language
Congruent phrases
Discernable structure

The world is not a poem
With its sculpted imagery
Its unified feeling
Its crystal clear themes

The world is not a poem
Even its ugliness beautiful
Its ignorance didactic
Its losses triumphant to a crescendo

The world is not a poem
It is rarely tranquil and gentle
Sometimes sadly unreal
Often too much to swallow
Always...

The world is not a poem...

Machete:

Used to only see it wrap up in a paper bag
So ya couldn't even see it.
Ya wouldn't even know it.
Brown bag to brown soil directly
Then back to brown bag.
Still, ya couldn't even see it.
The Haitian Excalibur.
Tucked in tight on the lawnmower's hip.
Mostly outta sight.

Gone from cutting weed
And chappin' bush
Limb by limb,
To chapping enemy and friend
Limb from limb,
Limb to limb,
Ear to ear,
Head to toe,
Ain tired yet..
Tooth for a tooth,
Eye for an eye.
Aye.
For no reason.
Chappin' and chappin',
Costin' this country an arm and a leg.

|47

A Marbled Sea:

She lies there.
Smooth skin suggesting depths of calm.
Soothing seas,
With which to be bathed, and washed over
In which to be baptized, and made clean.
Pure
And clear.
Perfect
And warm,
Reflecting the sun.

She lies there
Basking,
Almost motionless,
Almost asleep.
Barely rising and falling through waves of gentle breath.

She lies there.
Calm,
Pristine.
We call her "calm" when she lies there.
We call her "serene".

But her heart does beat in waves,
And pound,
And pulse.
Washing in and out.

The waves do rise with her tantrums
Fists pounding the earth,
Punching,
Beating the sand;
Pulses rising.

Like spray,
Like steam,
And mist;
Clouds form a thin, white robe about her
Too loosely tied
Coming undone.

She is salty
Also sultry,
And slutty for certain.
With night drawing,
And dragging,
And tugging its curtain
Her bosom swelling against the shoreline
She lies there in the waning light,
Swelling in waves of anticipation
In waves of darkness washing in.

As she thinks not of baptisms,
But of herself
And sin;
Suggestive, seductive whispers
Sound like a gentle breeze.

She lies there,
The white ribbons of her nightie
Long thrown open to the heavens,
Unclasped
Blowing in the wind.
She, her lover's muse,
Basking in the light of the marbled moon
Aglow and glistening,
As he descends into the depths
From full moon
To half.
Waist deep,
And deepening.
Submerged
Stirring currents under the surface
Under the cover of darkness.
Setting
And settling in.
She swells,
Swallowing light.

She, who once religiously bore the weight of miracles
Two of everything,
And the two feet of a Messiah,

Afloat, Atop a Marbled Sea

Now faithfully parting;
But not for Moses...

Propped up against the walls of night,
And at once clutching the horizon and the shore
Her skirt is pulled back in rising tides.
Exposing edges of ivory lace and frills
Fraying from being dragged along sand and rocks
Being grabbed and pulled up in the dark,
Still white and soft as sea foam.

She rises in wicked waves to meet him,
Rocking back and forth.
Splashing up against the night
In violent and stormy swells
Under blushing, blinking stars.

At times like this, the dawn seems so far away.
But when it comes, she pulls away,
She's all alone.
Gathering herself
50| Drawing into herself.
Dragging,
Pulling tight the strings of her see-through robe
As if not fully exposed to God's daylight.

What threads of shame there sometimes are,
Thin and frayed,
Wash out with the tide,
And will be long forgotten by the noon;
By then, long forgotten by the moon.
Left practically naked,
Vulnerable,
And for a time, low
On a disheveled bed.

But she is so many things, even by day.
The subtle curves of her warmth, smoothness of her skin
Begs others in,
If only for a dip.
Not knowing of all the others before,
The others to come;

And not long ago,
And not far away;
All riding new and "virgin" waves.
No wonder she is a mother,
Herself a womb,
Swells,
As does her bosom
Giving and sustaining life.
Sometimes contracting,
Often convulsing,
Expelling what she will not drown.

She is also a tomb
Miles out,
Miles wide,
Miles deep,
Unmarked.
A watery graveyard,
Murderous and treacherous
Lying in wait.

Even to be caught,
To be overcome,
Is to sometimes be unaware;
To be washed over
With soft and gentle strokes,
Until rough edges turn smooth
And still.
Even the petrified thing,
Polished down to a marbled mirror
Revealing all of her faces.

She is certainly a criminal
Aiding and abetting hurricane henchmen.
And sharks.
Fueling frenzies
Showered in ill-gotten gains,
Drenched
In rum-running,
Dope-dealing.

Afloat, Atop a Marbled Sea

Complicit in ship-wrecking,
Yet, keeping pirates afloat,
And slave ships;
Certainly wetting the wheels of Slavery
And whetting its knives.
While wrecking,
Dashing black lives and livelihoods against ship-wrecking rocks.

White-washing its guilt and guile,
Washing away crimes scenes,
A crime scene herself;
Certainly a criminal,
Her bloodguilt the only thing she can't wash clean.

Instead,
She washes away sandcastles
And beach balls.
Sometimes sand,
And beaches;
Certainly footprints,
As if life never came this way...
Certainly bridges,
Connecting islands she has made.

When she is petty,
The smaller they all become.
Islands
Worn down bit by bit
Day by day.
Making them more alone.
Farther apart.
Further adrift.

Afloat,
Atop a marbled sea...

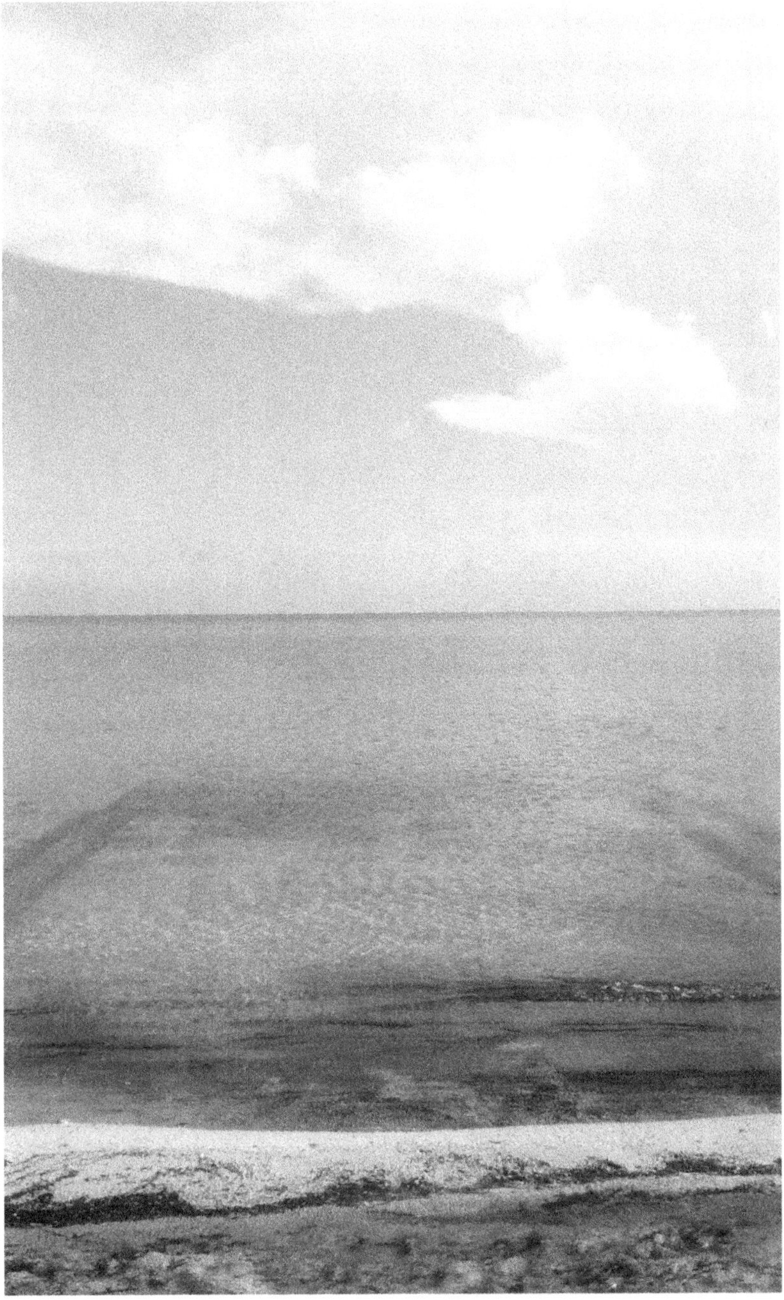

Afloat, Atop a Marbled Sea

54|

Afloat, Atop a Marbled Sea

Kenyada S. Meadows

Read numbers. Paint words.

Afloat, Atop a Marbled Sea

Afloat, Atop a Marbled Sea